Bionics

Judith Jango-Cohen

LERNER PUBLICATIONS COMPANY
MINNEAPOLIS

To my bionic brother Bob, with all my love

The author thanks the many people who shared their
stories, including Lyn Kolsteren, Shannon Barefield,
Dale Hylton, Dora Jango, and Grace Jango.
Thanks also to Joelle Riley, editor—a wonderful partner,
who brings out my best.

Text copyright © 2007 by Judith Jango-Cohen

Lerner Publications Company
A division of Lerner Publishing Group
241 First Avenue North
Minneapolis, MN 55401 U.S.A.

Website address: www.lernerbooks.com

Library of Congress Cataloging-in-Publication Data

Jango-Cohen, Judith.
    Bionics / by Judith Jango-Cohen.
       p.   cm. — (Cool science)
    Includes bibliographical references and index.
    ISBN-13: 978-0-8225-5937-5 (lib. bdg. : alk. paper)
    ISBN-10: 0-8225-5937-4 (lib. bdg. : alk. paper)
    1. Bionics—Juvenile literature. 2. Prosthesis—Juvenile literature. 3. Biomedical engineering—Juvenile
literature. I. Title. II. Series.
    Q320.5.J36 2007
    617′.9—dc22
                                                2005032221

Manufactured in the United States of America
1 2 3 4 5 6 – BP – 12 11 10 09 08 07

Table of Contents

Introduction

The lovable Tin Man and the hateful Captain Hook have something in common. They are both bionic. Each is a living being with artificial body parts. The Tin Man has a metal body. But he didn't start out that way. A witch cast a spell on his ax. The enchanted ax kept slipping and injuring him. So a tinsmith made metal replacements for his body parts. Captain Hook has an iron hook for a hand. He lost his own hand in a sword fight with Peter Pan.

Bionic people also live outside of storybooks and movies. About 10 percent of Americans have artificial devices attached to their bodies or implanted inside them. Doctors, scientists, and engineers work together to create these bionic devices.

Captain Hook was bionic because he had a hook for a hand.

4

Bionic devices serve different purposes. Some replace body parts that are missing due to injury, disease, or birth defects. For example, a person may lose a nose tip during cancer surgery. A new, bionic nose tip made of lifelike rubbery "skin" can replace it.

Other bionic devices help body parts that do not work properly. Tiny metal tubes called stents keep clogged blood vessels open. Devices embedded in the ear pick up sounds for people who can't hear.

In the future, people may use bionic devices to improve healthy bodies. Scientists are developing strap-on robotic legs. The legs will help firefighters and soldiers carry heavy loads. With the bionic legs, a 100-pound (45 kilograms) load feels like 5 pounds (2 kg). Zoom lenses may one day be added to people's eyes. They would work like telescopes to see distant objects. Or they could magnify tiny things, as microscopes do.

For centuries, people have dreamed of repairing and improving their bodies with bionic inventions. Some of their wildest dreams have become reality.

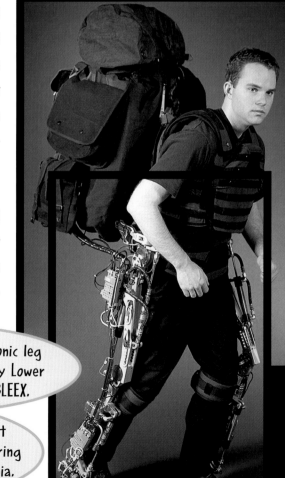

This man is demonstrating bionic leg technology called the Berkeley Lower Extremity Exoskeleton, or BLEEX.

BLEEX is being developed by scientists at the Berkeley Robotics and Human Engineering Laboratory at the University of California.

chapter 1

Replacing Parts

Bionics is not a modern idea. Old myths tell of bionic heroes and gods. The Norse god Thor the Thunderer had iron gloves. They helped him lift and crush boulders. He also wore a belt that doubled his strength. Other myths tell of Thor's wife, Sif. A prank-playing god destroyed Sif's lovely hair. But elves made new hair from fine golden threads. The golden hair grew on Sif's head thereafter.

Many recent stories feature bionic villains. Darth Vader, of the *Star Wars* movies, was badly wounded in a fight with Obi-Wan Kenobi. As a result, Lord Vader is part man and part machine. He has mechanical arms and legs and a bionic breathing device.

Fiction is full of bionic superheroes and villians, such as the evil Darth Vader.

Bionic Horse

Thor, the horse, is bionic—just like the Nordic god of the same name. His bionic device is an artificial leg. Thor's right rear leg was mangled when he caught it in some wire. Thor's veterinarian discussed the problem with a man who makes artificial legs for people. Soon Thor had a new leg.

Thor travels to children's hospitals. He visits kids who need artificial arms or legs.

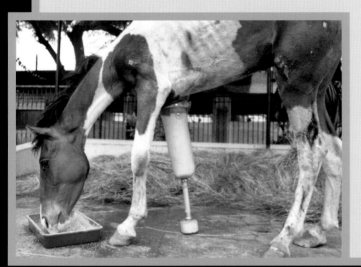

He also visits Adventure Camp, in Middleburg, Virginia. This is a camp for children who have lost a limb. In his spare time, Thor plays, bucks, and chases the lady horses around.

Macho, a horse from Bombay, India, is another horse fitted with an artificial leg.

In the film *Spider-Man 2*, Dr. Otto Octavius becomes Dr. Octopus when an experiment goes horribly wrong. Four metal arms become fused to his spinal cord. This writhing monster of a man then terrorizes the city.

The Real Deal

Long ago, people's imaginations created amazing bionic devices, such as clothing that magnifies muscle power. But until the twentieth century, bionic devices simply replaced missing parts. Ancient Egyptians carved false teeth that could be implanted into the jaw. They made the teeth out of ivory, bone, or seashells. But most early replacement parts were not natural looking. A French army surgeon in the 1500s invented artificial eyes made of gold or silver. Wax was used to replace facial features, such as a nose sliced off in a sword fight. The first bionic limbs were peg legs (stiff wooden posts) and wooden arms with iron hooks for hands.

These illustrations from a 1791 American book show two types of artificial legs available then, including a peg leg (lower right).

A 4,000-year-old Indian sacred poem, the *Rig-Veda*, is the oldest known account of an artificial limb. The poem tells of Queen Vishpla, who lost one of her legs during a battle. The queen was not discouraged. She returned to war wearing an iron leg.

Another bionic story describes a German knight, Götz von Berlichingen. In 1504, he lost a hand when a cannon misfired. A craftsman made him a metal hand. The hand had spring-operated fingers that let him hold a sword. The bionic knight became known as Götz of the Iron Hand.

Armorlike artificial legs were also made for knights. Bendable knee joints allowed them to sit properly on their horses. Strings ran from a waist belt to the knee joints. The knights bent the joints by pulling the strings.

In the 1800s, cable-controlled arms were developed. A 1915 magazine story describes wooden arms with steel joints. Leather cords stretched from elastic suspenders to elbows and fingers. Shrugging the shoulders stretched the suspenders and pulled the cords. In this way, the wearer could bend an elbow or open a hand.

Some people became whizzes at using these shoulder-powered limbs. One man, who had lost both his arms, amazed a group of surgeons. He could tie his scarf, button his shirt, and put on his coat. He could even pour himself a drink—without spilling it!

Electric Limbs

Some people never got the knack of using the cable-controlled arm. Some disliked the bulky cords. Others felt embarrassed because people stared when they shrugged their shoulders to move the arm.

In the 1970s, the myoelectric (electronic) arm was introduced. Moving muscles make electrical signals. The arm taps into these signals. To operate the arm, the person thinks about moving a finger or elbow. The brain then sends signals along nerves to the stump of the person's natural arm. These nerves make the muscles contract (tighten). Sensors on the arm pick up the electrical signals these contracting muscles make. The sensors pass the signals to microprocessors (tiny computer chips) in the artificial arm. The microprocessors "read" the signals. The signals then turn on motors in the bionic elbow, wrist, or fingers.

The Utah Arm is a commonly used myoelectric arm. It was developed at the University of Utah.

Despite its sensors, microprocessors, batteries, and motors, the myoelectric arm is not bulky. The motors, computer chips, and batteries are all built-in. The sensors can be placed on the skin over the muscles. They can also be implanted in the end of the artificial arm. These parts can be made small enough to fit into a young child's tiny limb.

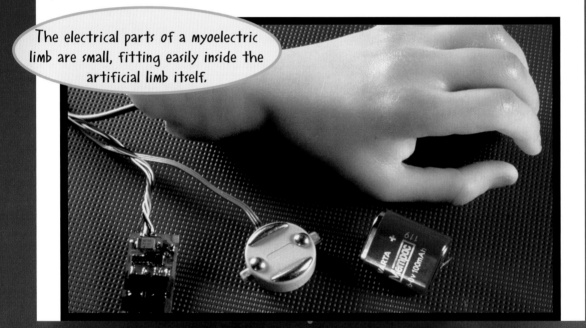

The electrical parts of a myoelectric limb are small, fitting easily inside the artificial limb itself.

The Latest Legs

Myoelectric arms need to make fine movements. They need to be able to turn pages and twist bottle tops. Technology for artificial legs focuses on strength, speed, smooth movement, and balance. Lightweight but strong materials have replaced iron and wood. Many artificial legs contain carbon fiber. This material is also used to make jets, tennis rackets, and golf clubs. Titanium, found in computers and cars, is another popular material. Titanium weighs about half as much as steel but is just as strong.

Hand-Me-Down Arms

Kids grow quickly. Parents groan at the cost of replacing their outgrown clothing. But how about when a child outgrows an expensive myoelectric arm? The Myoelectric Limb Bank has come to the rescue. Children can bring an old arm to the limb bank. They can trade it for a used arm that's bigger. The arm's socket must be custom-fitted for the new owner. Children also get hands designed for their needs. For example, a girl who plays softball needs a hand that can fit into a ball glove. Another child may need to hold a drumstick. Because of these adjustments, the used arm may still cost a few thousand dollars. If the parents cannot pay the whole cost, the limb bank "gives them a hand."

Some of the most popular bionic devices have been designed by people who use them. Van Phillips lost his foot in a waterskiing accident. A boat's propeller cut it off. He didn't like the available replacements, so he designed his own. His strong but flexible carbon-fiber invention comes in several varieties. He has made feet for mountain climbers and for bike riders. Phillips is also working on an adaptable foot. It will let people jog one minute and play golf the next.

Artificial limbs allow people who have lost their own limbs to continue to play the sports they enjoy.

Hugh Herr lost both legs to frost-bite while climbing New Hampshire's Mount Washington. He was only 17. He was not about to let his disability keep him down. He invented a spring-loaded foot for easier walking. He also designed feet for climbers. One model is narrow, so it can fit into rock crevices. Another has spikes for climbing over ice.

Hugh Herr poses with an artificial leg. Since his accident, Herr has worked toward improving the design of artificial knees and feet.

Titanium Attachments

Artificial limbs have a hollow socket that fits onto the body. Suction or straps hold the socket in place. The socket is custom-made for each person's body. But wearing an artificial limb can be uncomfortable. In hot weather, the socket gets sweaty. It can cause a rash. And the body's tissues shrink and swell throughout the day. As they do, the socket becomes tighter or looser. It rubs against the skin, causing blisters.

Researchers are developing a way to avoid these problems. They are linking limbs directly to the body. Scientists have conducted

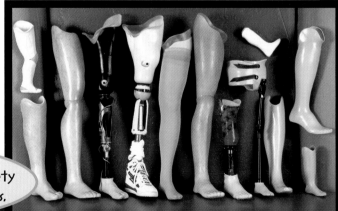

Artificial limbs come in a variety of sizes, shapes, and materials.

the first experiments with artificial legs. A surgeon implants a titanium bolt into the end of the remaining leg bone. The person's bone cells begin to grow onto the titanium. After six months, the bolt is securely anchored. At this point, the surgeon adds a titanium attachment piece. Then the wearer can screw on an artificial leg.

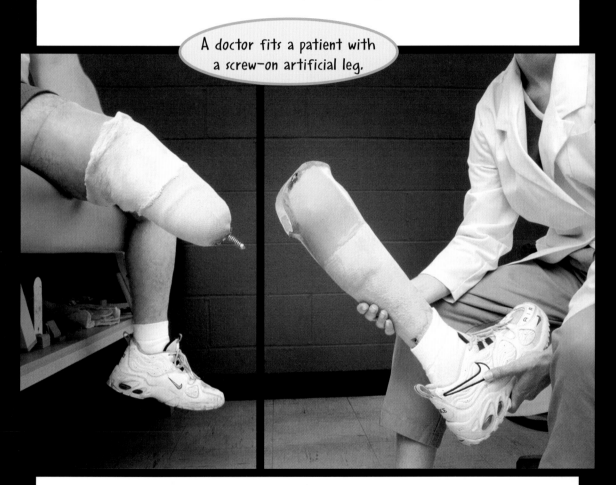

A doctor fits a patient with a screw-on artificial leg.

This screw-on leg is a great improvement. There is no rubbing from a bad fit. Leg muscles can control the bone to which the artificial leg is connected. Because it is part of the body, people use less energy to move with it. It is not deadweight to be lugged around. People like being able to sense where the leg is in space. They can also feel the surface they are walking on. Walking on grass feels different from walking on concrete.

Arm implants may be possible one day as well. Scientists have already developed implanted thumbs. The thumb screws onto the bone in a person's hand.

Detector Dilemma

Artificial limbs and joints sometimes set off airport metal detectors. Some people with artificial limbs or joints carry a medical card. The card explains that they need to be checked by hand. One woman found a quicker way around the problem. She just removes her leg. After handing it to the inspector, she hops through the detector.

New Knuckles and Knees

Some people do not need a new leg or arm. Instead, they need a new joint. Replacement of knees, knuckles, elbows, and hips has become routine. Knees and hips are the most commonly replaced joints.

Why would someone need a new joint? Athletes often have accidents that cause joint injuries. Their joints also suffer from wear and tear. Repeated motions, such as pitching a ball or swinging a tennis racket, can damage joints.

Arthritis is another culprit. In a healthy joint, a tough material called cartilage helps bones slide smoothly when the joint bends. One kind of arthritis wears away this cartilage. When the cartilage breaks down, bone rubs against bone. Moving the joint becomes painful. Another form of arthritis makes joints crooked, stiff, and swollen. A new artificial joint may be the solution.

Surgeons remove the damaged parts, then implant the new joint. The replacement joint is usually made of two pieces. One part is made of titanium or stainless steel. This metal piece fits into another piece made of tough plastic. After a few weeks or months of healing, the new joint restores smooth movement.

Artificial knees (left) and hips (right) are the most commonly implanted bionic joints.

Bionic joints and limbs help people have a satisfying life. They get out and jog, ski, and even climb mountains. A missing body part is not a setback. It is just a challenge to be met.

chapter 2

Fixing Malfunctions

Rica and Derrick Walker named their son Kerrick. The name means "warrior." They chose it because Kerrick was battling for his life even before he was born.

Doctors discovered that Rica's unborn child's heartbeat was too slow. The heart pumps blood through the body. The blood carries oxygen that the body's cells need to stay alive. But Kerrick's cells were not getting enough oxygen.

A normal newborn's heart beats about 120 times per minute. Kerrick's heart rate was only 40 beats per minute. To speed up

This infant's heartbeat is being monitored by an electrode on its chest.

Kerrick's heart, doctors gave his mother medicine. This kept Kerrick alive until he was born. Then he became a bionic baby.

Setting the Pace

Normally a part of the heart called the sinus node controls the heartbeat. The sinus node acts like a switch. When this switch turns on, an electrical signal spreads through the heart. The signal makes the heart beat. Kerrick's sinus node wasn't working right. Surgeons implanted a pacemaker just below Kerrick's chest. This device would set the pace for Kerrick's heart rate.

Kerrick's pacemaker is about the size of a quarter. It contains a tiny battery. Electrical signals from the pacemaker travel through wires to Kerrick's heart. The electrical signals keep his heart beating normally. When he is older, Kerrick will receive a larger pacemaker.

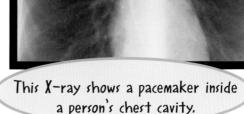

This X-ray shows a pacemaker inside a person's chest cavity.

Pacemakers help people who have a slow or unsteady heartbeat. But some people's hearts beat too fast. A person's heart speeds up when a heart attack or disease has damaged it. The weakened heart cannot pump hard enough.

The heart has two bottom pumping chambers called ventricles. Sometimes the ventricles beat out of rhythm with each other. The heart struggles. It beats faster to try to move enough oxygen through the body. This tires the already worn-out heart.

How the Heart Works

Each side of the heart has two main parts—an atrium and a ventricle. When the atrium fills with blood, a valve opens. Blood rushes from the atrium into the ventricle. Then the ventricle pushes the blood out into the body.

The right and left sides of the heart have different jobs. The right side receives oxygen-poor blood from the body and pumps it to the lungs. In the lungs, oxygen enters the blood. The oxygen-rich blood from the lungs flows into the left side of the heart. Then the heart pumps it through the body.

to the head and arms

from the head and arms

to the right lung

from the right lung

to the left lung

from the left lung

sinus node

left atrium

right atrium

LEFT SIDE

RIGHT SIDE

left ventricle

oxygen-poor blood

oxygen-rich blood

right ventricle

from the lower body

to the lower body

A resynchronizer can help the heart work better. This device produces electrical signals that slow the heart down. These signals also resynchronize the heartbeat. They keep the ventricles beating in synch with each other. This helps the heart to pump more blood with each beat.

Battery Check

After a while, batteries die. But people can't risk having their implanted pacemaker batteries conk out. To prevent this, a signal goes off six months before the batteries need replacing. The operation to replace the batteries takes a few hours. The person returns home the same day. Fortunately, these batteries last up to 10 years.

A Bionic Safety Net

Severe heart attacks may damage much of the heart's tissue. Then a heart transplant becomes necessary. Doctors replace the damaged heart with the heart of a person who has died.

In the United States, about 8,000 people need a heart transplant each year. But only 2,000 hearts become available each year. People may have to wait a year or more for a transplant. What if a person's heart will not hold out that long?

A device called the CardioWest Total Artificial Heart can help. The CardioWest takes over the job of the two ventricles—the business end of the heart. The ventricles fill with blood from the two atria above them. Then the ventricles pump the blood out.

Before implanting the CardioWest, the surgeon removes the person's damaged ventricles. Then the CardioWest's two pumping chambers are attached to the remaining heart. Air pressure pushes blood out of these chambers. The air is driven by a computerized pumping machine. Tubes connect this machine to the person's body.

With a healthy blood flow, people can stay strong while waiting for a transplant. Scientists

The CardioWest Total Artificial Heart

conducted a study of the CardioWest from 1993 to 2002. During that time, 79 percent of people with a CardioWest heart lived long enough to receive a transplant. Only 46 percent survived without the CardioWest. Some people in France have lived with the bionic device for more than three years.

The pumping machine is big. People on the CardioWest cannot leave the hospital. But in Europe, researchers are developing smaller drivers. These pumps can be implanted into the body. The researchers' goal is for the CardioWest to become a permanent artificial heart. This could be a bionic blessing for nearly five million Americans suffering from heart failure.

A CardioWest Success

Bill Wohl has had three hearts. He lived with his own heart until a massive heart attack left it too crippled to function. Heart number two was a CardioWest device. Bill stayed active while connected to this 400-pound (180 kg) pumper. He even worked out in the hospital gym. After 159 days, heart number three—a transplant— became available. With his new heart, Bill was able to exercise more and rebuild his body. He has competed at international athletic events, such as the World Transplant Games. Bill has won medals in cycling, swimming, and track events. "He had the right attitude," says his surgeon. "Never give up."

Bill Wohl was featured in the January 7, 2005, issue of Life magazine.

Special Health Preview 2005

LIFE

25 Health Breakthroughs That Will Change Your Life

Meet Bill Wohl. He's a successful businessman, a champion cyclist.
Would you believe this man's had three hearts?

The Next Diet Pill? • An Easier Way to Quit Smoking • Help for an Aching Back   WEEKEND OF JANUARY **7** 2005

Dealing with Diabetes

Heart disease afflicts mostly older people. But diabetes affects people of all ages. There are two kinds of diabetes. Type 2 diabetes shows up most often in adults. But Type 1 diabetes usually flares up in children and teenagers.

The body breaks down most of the food we eat into a sugar called glucose. The hormone insulin brings glucose into the body's cells, which burn it for energy. The pancreas is the organ that produces insulin. It releases insulin throughout the day. The pancreas adjusts its production of insulin to match the amount of glucose in the blood. So after a meal, the pancreas revs up its production.

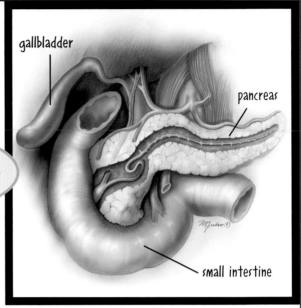

gallbladder

pancreas

small intestine

The pancreas is found near the part of the small intestine that is attached to the stomach.

People with Type 1 diabetes make little or no insulin. Without enough insulin, glucose cannot enter the cells. Instead, it builds up in the blood. Over time, high glucose blood levels can cause serious health problems. To prevent this, people with Type 1 diabetes inject insulin into their blood. Many diabetics give themselves shots to inject the insulin. They have to time the shots with regularly scheduled meals. Too much glucose in the blood can cause shortness of breath and vomiting. Too little glucose can cause dizziness. Keeping a strict schedule is important. But it can also be difficult.

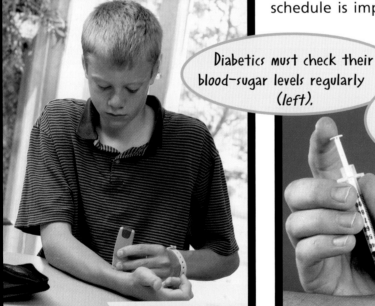

Diabetics must check their blood-sugar levels regularly (left).

Diabetics inject themselves with insulin (below) when there is too much glucose in their blood.

A Portable Pancreas

Fortunately, a bionic device can help many people with Type 1 diabetes. It is a pump that imitates the way the pancreas works.

The insulin pump is about the size of a beeper. Tubing connects it to the body. Diabetics can wear the pump on a belt or in a pouch on the upper leg. A five-week-old baby had the pump attached to her diaper. If needed, a hard, watertight case can be snapped on. This protects the pump while a person plays, swims, or bathes.

The pump holds insulin. The insulin travels into the body through the tubing. Like the real pancreas, the pump delivers a steady flow of insulin throughout the day. This is more natural than the few large doses delivered through shots. It is also healthier, because glucose is delivered to the cells more regularly. Different people need different amounts of insulin. The amount required depends on how much insulin a person's body is making. It also depends upon a person's size, age, and health. But the pump can be programmed to deliver the proper rate of insulin.

Unfortunately, the bionic pancreas cannot fine-tune its insulin production as a

IT'S A FACT!

In 2000, 10–day–old Maverick Roe became the youngest person ever to receive an insulin pump.

Golfer Michelle McGann (right) wore her insulin pump to the 2002 Kraft Nabisco Championship.

real pancreas does. Wearers must set the insulin pump themselves during meals and exercise. If someone craves a midnight snack, the pump must be set to deliver more insulin. Before taking a bike ride, a person must program the pump to slow down its delivery. Exercise reduces the amount of glucose in the blood, so less insulin is required.

Pump Pockets

Wearing an insulin pump has become more fashionable thanks to Pump Wear, Inc. Julie DeFruscio founded the company after her three-year-old daughter, Nikki, developed diabetes. Neither Nikki nor her mother liked the bulky harness that held Nikki's pump. But the pump had to be kept out of Nikki's reach. Otherwise, she could play with the controls and set them for a dangerous amount of insulin. Julie had a back pocket sewn into Nikki's shirts. Soon the idea for a clothing company developed. The company designs pants, pajamas, shirts, and shorts with hidden insulin-pump pockets. Slits behind the pockets allow the tubing to go through. It also makes belts with a pouch for the pump. Being bionic never looked so good.

Eight-year-old Nikki Tyler DeFruscio (right) has Type 1 diabetes. She wears an insulin pump she can stash in her stylish Pump Wear, Inc., clothes.

Thumper the Pump

People are physically attached to their insulin pumps. But they often become emotionally attached as well. A children's book editor named her pump Charlotte, after the spider in *Charlotte's Web*. Other pump names include Annie, Kramer, and Thumper.

People who wear an insulin pump love the freedom it gives them. They can stay in bed if they want to, instead of having to get up for an injection. If they are playing baseball, they don't have to leave the game to take their shot. They don't have to eat at particular times. The insulin pump frees people to have fun.

chapter 3

Assisting the Senses

Lyn Kolsteren felt bombarded by sounds. Dishes clattered in the kitchen. Her son's pen squeaked across the dry-erase board. The quick footsteps of her baby patted down the hall. And through an open window, a bird sang. Lyn was thrilled.

This world of sounds was new to Lyn. She had been born with defects in both ears that caused hearing loss. Lyn could hear sounds only if they were just a few feet away. In school, she could not hear the teacher. She remembers being told to sit down and stop asking questions. The work had already been explained.

Chain Reaction

Because of the defects in Lyn's ears, sounds could not follow their normal pathway. This pathway begins in the outer ear and ends in the brain. When sounds enter the outer ear, they travel down the ear canal and hit the eardrum. This causes the eardrum to vibrate. These vibrations travel to three tiny bones in the middle ear. All three bones could fit on one of your fingernails. These vibrating bones amplify (strengthen) the sound and send it to the inner ear.

The inner ear contains a snail-shaped structure called the cochlea. Special cells called hair cells line the inside of the cochlea. It is filled with fluid. Sound waves travel through this fluid. As they do so, they wiggle the tips of hair cells. Different hair cells are sensitive to sounds with different pitches. Some vibrate to high sounds, others to low sounds. Loud noises make bigger waves in the fluid than soft ones. They push harder on the hair cells.

IT'S A FACT!
The cochlea has 20,000 hair cells.

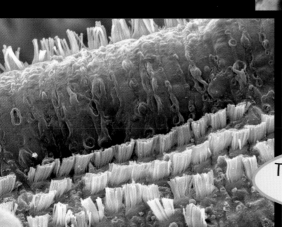

The cochlea (*above*) is snail shaped and lined with thousands of tiny hair cells (*left*).

When the cochlea's hair cells vibrate, they produce electrical signals. These signals travel to the auditory (hearing) nerve. The auditory nerve passes the signals on to the brain. The brain decodes the signals it receives as high, low, soft, or loud sounds.

Parts of the Ear

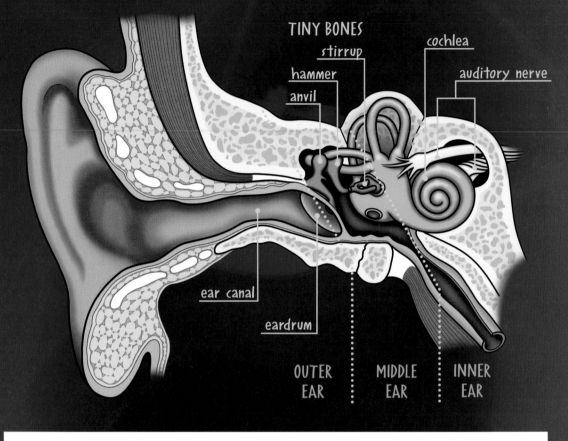

TINY BONES
stirrup
hammer
anvil
cochlea
auditory nerve
ear canal
eardrum

OUTER EAR • MIDDLE EAR • INNER EAR

As people age, the hair cells in the cochlea may die or become damaged. Ear infections, loud noises, and injuries may also damage these cells. Often a hearing aid worn in the outer ear can help. Hearing aids amplify incoming sounds.

But some people, like Lyn, cannot be helped by hearing aids. This is because parts of their outer and middle ears do not work properly. Sound cannot be passed along if the pathway is broken.

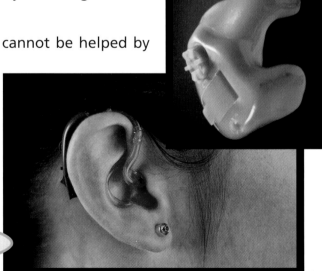

Traditional hearing aids

Bionic Bypass

A bionic device can bypass the areas of the ear that are "out of order." A bone-anchored hearing aid (BAHA) can deliver sounds directly to the inner ear. The device is implanted in the skull. A tiny screw is embedded into the bone behind the ear. After the skull bone heals, a receiver is attached. The receiver picks up sounds.

The sounds travel through the screw and the skull bones and on to the inner ear.

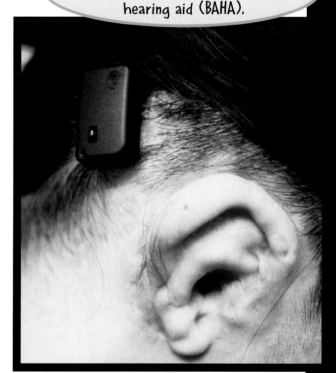

This man shows off his bone-anchored hearing aid (BAHA).

Lyn was nervous about having the BAHA implanted. She was queasy about having "a bolt in her head." But she went through with the surgery. Lyn loves her "magic ear," as her three-year-old daughter calls it. "If sound were colors," Lyn says, "I would describe the BAHA to be a professional artist's paint box with 10 shades per color."

Unplugged

You're wrestling with a math problem, but your little brother keeps screeching. Outside, your puppy is yapping at a visiting raccoon. What do you do? If you are wearing a BAHA, there is no problem. Just remove or turn off the receiver and go "unplugged" for a while. Ahh... the comfort of quiet!

The BAHA relies on a working inner ear. People with defects or damage to the cochlea need a different solution. A device implanted in the cochlea can often help. Like the BAHA, a cochlear implant detours around nonfunctioning areas. It bypasses the outer, middle, and inner ear. It delivers sound directly to the auditory nerve. The cochlear implant has both external and internal parts. The external parts detect and transmit sounds. The internal parts deliver these signals to the auditory nerve.

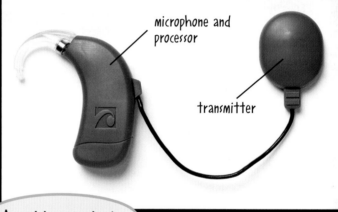

microphone and processor

transmitter

A cochlear implant

The cochlear implant includes a tiny, external microphone. The microphone picks up sounds. It delivers them to a battery-powered computer processor. The processor changes these sounds into electrical signals. A thin cable then carries the signals to a transmitter. The transmitter sends the signals to a receiver embedded in the skull. Wires connect the receiver to the cochlea. When the electrical signals reach the cochlea, they stimulate the auditory nerve. Nerve impulses then travel to the brain and the person can "hear."

A person with a cochlear implant cannot hear as well as a person with normal hearing. The processor cannot produce as many different types of signals as the cochlea. One person describes the implant's sounds as "squeaky or tinny, like Minnie Mouse." But the cochlear implant works well enough to let people talk with family and friends. Some can even use the telephone. Phone conversations are more difficult, though. The listener cannot use lipreading as a backup.

A scientist poses with a display of a bionic ear, the Nucleus Freedom, in 2005.

This bionic implant allows deaf people to hear clearly, even in crowds and other noisy environments.

Cochlear implants and the BAHA make people feel more connected to the world. They improve a person's ability to communicate. Sharing feelings and ideas is a need all human beings have.

Cloudy Eyes

Besides hearing, another sense that people rely upon is sight. In order for us to see, light must enter the eye through the cornea. The cornea partly focuses the light before it passes through the pupil. Light entering the pupil next travels through the lens. The lens fine-tunes the focus. The focused light reaches the back of the eye, called the retina. Cells in the retina change the light into electrical signals. These signals then travel through the optic nerve and to the brain.

Parts of the Eye

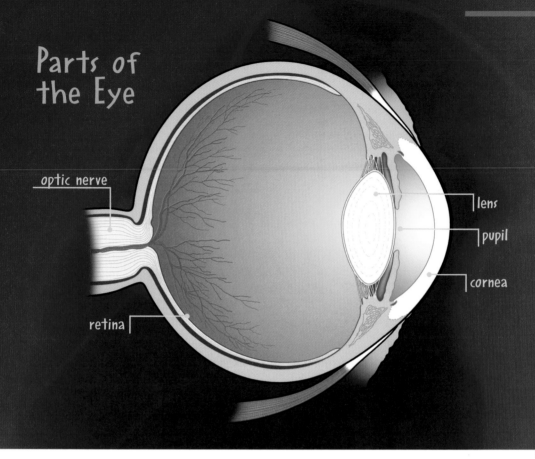

optic nerve

retina

lens

pupil

cornea

Unfortunately, many eye diseases and injuries lead to permanent loss of sight. But one common problem—cataracts—has a bionic solution. Cataracts form on the lens of the eye. They make the normally clear lens cloudy. The cloudy lens blocks the light instead of allowing it to pass through. With time, cataracts can lead to complete blindness. Cataracts may result from disease or injury. Some babies are born with them. But aging causes most cataracts.

IT'S A FACT!
Every year, about one million Americans have their sight restored with cataract surgery.

A Lens Implant

To treat cataracts, the clouded lens must be removed. This is usually done in a 10- to 30-minute operation. The person can go home shortly afterward. Before the operation, a surgeon numbs the eye. Then the surgeon cuts a tiny hole in the cornea. High-frequency sound waves (sounds too high for us to hear) are used to shatter the center of the cataract. The surgeon then suctions out the fragments. A small plastic lens is compressed and inserted through the incision. The lens unfolds inside the eye.

The bionic lens works the way the natural lens does—with one difference. The artificial lens is not as flexible as the real one. It cannot change shape as well to focus on both near and faraway objects. So after cataract surgery, people may need to wear glasses or contacts.

In the late 1990s, multifocal lenses became available. These lenses can focus at different distances. For some people, multifocal lenses decrease or eliminate the need for glasses after cataract surgery. But others don't like them. They find that these lenses produce annoying halos around lights at night.

A Visionary

Before lens implants were invented, people had to wear thick eyeglasses after cataract surgery. Besides being unsightly, the lenses did not provide good side vision. A British surgeon named Harold Ridley came upon the idea of lens implants. The idea came to him while treating World War II pilots in the 1940s. Some of these pilots had pieces of plastic from broken windshields embedded in their eyes. Ridley noticed that the plastic did not cause irritation. He reasoned that the eye could tolerate plastic lens implants. Dr. Ridley's idea was ridiculed at first. But in the 1970s, it began to gain acceptance. In 2000, Queen Elizabeth II of England knighted Sir Harold Ridley for his "visionary" work.

Cataract Quotes

People who have had cataract surgery give good reports. "It's like having a new set of eyes," an artist says. "It was much easier to have the cataracts removed than to have a tooth pulled," says another. But, she sighs, there is a downside. She can see the crumbs on the counter, the hairs on the sink, and the dust on the desk. "I look a lot older now too," she adds. "When I look in the mirror I can see every wrinkle!"

This photo shows a pea-sized telescope being implanted into a person's eye.

The device was developed to help people with damaged retinas.

A Stimulating Experiment

Damage to the retina or optic nerve also causes vision loss. Such problems are harder to solve than cataracts. But scientists are finding ways to bypass diseased or injured areas of the eye. They are experimenting with direct stimulation of the retina, optic nerve, or brain.

In Australia, researchers are working on a way to stimulate damaged retinas. Their method involves removing a person's lens and replacing it with a dime-sized capsule. The capsule contains a silicon microchip. A camera, worn on a pair of eyeglasses, radios pictures to the microchip. The microchip turns these pictures into electronic signals. The signals travel through wires to the retina. Then they are relayed to the optic nerve and on to the vision center of the brain. The brain processes these signals as sight.

This device does not give people sharp vision. But wearers can distinguish light from darkness. They can make out movement and large objects, so they don't bump into things. Some people can even read large-print books.

The ability to restore vision and hearing was just a dream not long ago. Where will our dreams take us as we enter the future?

chapter 4

Facing the Future

In a laboratory, scientists watch a two-wheeled robot zigzagging around a ring. The robot has light sensors and a motor. The inside of the ring is lined with lights that flicker off and on. When a light flashes on, the robot zips toward it. When the light blinks off, the robot stops.

The robot is being controlled by a lump of tissue in a container. The tissue is part of the brain of a fish.

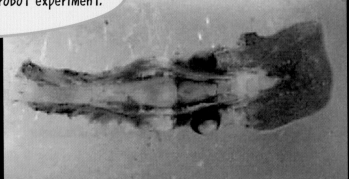

This brain tissue from a fish was used in the first thought-controlled robot experiment.

It is the section of the brain that controls vision, balance, and movement. Electrodes, which carry electrical current, are embedded in the brain tissue. Wires link the electrodes to the robot. When one of the robot's sensors detects light, it signals the electrodes in the brain. Brain neurons (nerve cells) return a signal telling the motor to move the robot toward the light.

Thought-Controlled

Experiments linking brains and machines may one day lead to thought-controlled bionic devices. Artificial limbs may be directed by brain signals, as natural ones are. The limbs may also be able to send feedback to the brain. Two-way communication would then be possible between the brain and the artificial limb. A hand may be able to signal the person that a glass is slippery and needs a stronger grip. It may also be able to tell the person that a cup is hot.

Brain implants may be able to control devices such as wheelchairs or cars. This could help people who are paralyzed. In 2004, scientists announced that a paralyzed man was able to move a computer cursor. Implanted electrodes sent brain signals to a computer as he thought about moving the cursor. The man was able to point to letters and spell out words. Similar technology may also help paralyzed people who cannot speak. Computers picking up signals from their brains may one day translate their thoughts into language.

In the future, brain implants may move paralyzed arms and legs. These limbs are paralyzed because nerves in the spinal cord are damaged. The nerves can no longer carry signals to the limbs. Signals from the brain implants will bypass the damaged nerves. The signals will be able to reach the limbs. This will allow the person to move once again.

Monkey Business

Monkeys are helping scientists create thought-controlled artificial limbs. In one experiment, researchers implanted electrodes into a monkey's brain. As the monkey moved its arm, its brain signals were sent to a computerized artificial arm. The computerized arm was hooked up to the Internet in another state. Nevertheless, the robotic limb moved right along with the real one.

Dr. Nicolelis of Duke University with an owl monkey and a computerized artificial arm

Nanobots

In the future, scientists may use bionics to repair damage and fight disease at a microscopic level. They are developing tiny machines called nanobots. These machines are only nanometers (billionths of a meter) long. Scientists are designing some nanobots for use inside the human body. Because they are microscopic, they will be able to go inside cells. These microscopic machines could mean healthier humans. Nanobots may one day scour out clogged blood vessels. The cleared vessels will restore

IT'S A FACT!
One human hair is about 80,000 nanometers wide.

blood flow through the body. Nanobots may carry drugs to selected cells. They may patrol the bloodstream and pounce on germs. Nanobots may even be able to attack tumors.

A film still from *Fantastic Voyage* shows miniaturized doctors inside a scientist's body.

IT'S A FACT!

The 1966 movie *Fantastic Voyage* features nanobot-sized surgeons. They travel through a scientist's body to destroy a blood clot.

Superhuman

Someday bionics may give us superhuman abilities. Do you have a bad seat at the ball game? Implanted lenses may let you see that close play at home plate. Is your dog ignoring your calls to come in at night? Heat-sensing lenses may be able to detect him cornering a raccoon.

Bionic devices may also make it possible for humans to live in new places. People may live comfortably under the sea. They may use artificial gills to get oxygen from the water, as fish do. Perhaps they will wear devices that receive and send ultrasonic sounds—sounds outside of our hearing range. Whales and porpoises use these sounds to communicate.

Intelligence could also get a bionic boost. Tiny computer chips implanted in the brain could hook humans up to the Internet. Downloading information would be fast and simple. Math facts wouldn't have to be memorized. Taking years to learn a foreign language would be ancient history. Sending messages from your implanted computer to your friend's might let you "read" each other's minds.

Perhaps one day, your memories could be stored in a computer chip in your brain. You could replay them exactly as they happened. All of your brain's contents could be downloaded onto a computer. You could have your entire mind on a backup disk.

Microchip Trip

Scientists have developed a microchip-equipped camera so tiny that a person can swallow it. The pill-sized camera cruises through the body, snapping pictures. In its eight-hour journey, 50,000 images are sent to a recorder worn on the person's belt. The recorded data helps doctors diagnose illnesses that are not detectable with X-rays and other tests. At the end of the trip, the pill comes out with the person's wastes. Mission accomplished!

A man (far left) prepares to swallow a microchip-equipped camera capsule (another camera is shown at near left). The capsule contains a camera, a light source, and a radio transmitter.

Questions to Consider

Human imaginings plus increased knowledge have led to devices that improve and prolong life. Scientists are proud of their accomplishments. But their work also humbles them. Their research reveals how much they don't know. Much about our own bodies remains a mystery.

But time slowly peels away one mystery after another. Bionic break-throughs bring up some interesting questions. Will developments such as nanobots be available to all? Or will only the rich be able to afford these life-extending devices? If people live longer, will we have room for every-one on this crowded planet? Will we need laws to limit how many children we can have? If all your memories were on a computer, would that computer have a conscious mind? Would it be a machine or a being with feelings? Would it be another you?

Are these questions worth thinking about? Bodies patrolled by nanobots and memories on computer files seem like science fiction, not fact. But all the pres-ent-day bionic devices we enjoy began as fantasies.

The questions we face change, as yesterday's dreams become reali-ties. In 1982, before a man was to receive an artificial heart, his wife asked if he would still be able to love her. This question no longer troubles us. But as bionics research continues and machines merge more with body and brain, the questions get more complicated. Soon we may come face-to-face with the most difficult question of all. What does it mean to be human?

In the future, nanobots may be used to attack and kill abnormal cells within the body, such as cancer cells, as shown in this computer-generated artwork.

Glossary

arthritis: pain, swelling, and stiffness of a joint

bionic: having artificial body parts

cataract: a clouded area of the lens of the eye that blocks light

cochlea: a structure in the inner ear that turns sound vibrations into electrical signals

cornea: the clear front area of the eye

diabetes: a disease in which the body does not properly control the amount of sugar in the blood

glucose: a sugar found in the blood that is the body's main source of energy

heart attack: damage to the heart that occurs when a blood vessel is blocked, keeping the heart from receiving enough oxygen

insulin: a chemical that brings the sugar glucose into the body's cells so they can burn it for energy

myoelectric: converting nerve impulses into an electric current that can power a motor to move an artificial arm or hand

nerves: bundles of fibers that carry impulses between the brain and other parts of the body

optic nerve: the nerve that carries impulses from the eye to the brain

pacemaker: a device implanted in the chest to keep the heart beating properly

pancreas: the organ in the body that produces insulin

pupil: the opening in the eye through which light passes

retina: light-sensitive nerve tissue lining the back of the eye

transplant: an operation in which a diseased organ (such as a heart) is removed and replaced with a healthy organ

Selected Bibliography

Amputee Coalition of America. *Resources for Amputees*. 2005. http://www.amputee-coalition.org (February 27, 2006).

BAHA Users Support (Kent). *The Patients BAHA Website*. 2005. http://www.baha-users-support.com (February 27, 2006).

Cauwels, Janice M. *The Body Shop: Bionic Revolutions in Medicine*. New York: Random House, 1986.

Copeland J. G., M. J. Slepian, et al. "Cardiac Replacement with a Total Artificial Heart as a Bridge to Transplantation." *New England Journal of Medicine* 351 (2004): 859-867.

Ezzell, Carol, and Glenn Zorpette. *Scientific American Presents: Your Bionic Future*. New York: Scientific American, Fall 1999.

Gregson, Ian. *Amputee Web Site*. 2005. http://www.amputee-online.com/amputee/amputee.html (February 27, 2006).

Halacy, Jr., D. S. *Cyborg: Evolution of the Superman*. New York: Harper & Row Publishers, 1965.

Jauhar, Sandeep. "The Artificial Heart." *New England Journal of Medicine* 350 (2004): 542–544.

Kelley, Jack. "Monkeys, Humans Get Brain-Driven Prostheses." *Discover*, January 2005, 45.

Northwestern University. *Prosthetics Research Laboratory and Rehabilitation Engineering Research Program*. 2005. http://www.medschool.northwestern.edu/depts/repoc/ (February 27, 2006).

Perkowitz, Sidney. *Digital People: From Bionic Humans to Androids*. Washington, DC: Joseph Henry Press, 2004.

Project Bionics. *Artificial Organs from Discovery to Clinical Use*. 2005. http://echo.gmu.edu/bionics/ (February 27, 2006).

Slepian, Marvin, and Bill Wohl, interviewd by Robin Young. *Here and Now*. PBS, January 24, 2005.

Weiss, Rick. "Nanomedicine's Promise Is Anything but Tiny." *Washington Post*, January 31, 2005, A8.

Further Reading and Websites

Abdallah, Hasan. *The Children's Heart Institute: Patient Education.*
http://www.childrensheartinstitute.org/educate/eduhome.htm
The Children's Heart Institute patient education page has lots of information about how the heart works.

Amputee Coalition of America. *Youth Activities Program.*
http://www.amputee-coalition.org/youth.html
The Amputee Coalition of America is a national, nonprofit educational organization representing people who have lost limbs. The Youth Activities Program page has information for young people, including the Youth Amputee E-Zine.

Animated Prosthetics, Inc. *News and Announcements.*
http://www.animatedprosthetics.com/frames.htm
This is the News and Announcements page for Animated Prosthetics, a company that specializes in prosthetic arms.

Beecroft, Simon. *Super Humans: A Beginner's Guide to Bionics.* Brookfield, CT: Copper Beech Books, 1998.

Center for Disability Information and Referral. *CeDIR's Disability Awareness Site for Youth.*
http://www.iidc.indiana.edu/cedir/kidsweb/
Have you ever wondered what it's like to have a disability? This site can answer some of your questions. It includes lists of books about disabilities, movies with characters who are disabled, and famous people with disabilities.

Cobb, Allan B. *The Bionic Human.* New York: The Rosen Publishing Group, Inc., 2003.

Hannemann, Brendan. *Kids Learn about Diabetes.*
http://www.kidslearnaboutdiabetes.org/
This website is packed with information about living with diabetes.

Johnson, Rebecca L. *Nanotechnology.* Minneapolis: Lerner Publications Company, 2006.

KidsHealth. *What's Hearing Loss?*
> http://kidshealth.org/kid/health_problems/sight/hearing_impairment.html
> This website has information about the different kinds of hearing loss and how people with hearing loss communicate.

National Federation of the Blind. *Questions from Kids about Blindness.*
> http://www.nfb.org/kids.htm
> Have you ever wondered how blind people choose which clothes to wear or find their way around? This Web page answers these questions and many more.

PBS. *NOVA Online: Cut to the Heart.*
> http://www.pbs.org/wgbh/nova/heart
> This is the companion website for the *NOVA* program "Cut to the Heart." It covers the history of heart surgery and some of the things that can go wrong with the heart. It includes an animation of how the heart pumps blood.

Presnall, Judith Janda. *Artificial Organs.* San Diego: Lucent Books, Inc., 1996.

Rosaler, Maxine. *Bionics.* Farmington Hills, MI: Blackbirch Press, 2003.

ThinkQuest. *Come to Your Senses.*
> http://library.thinkquest.org/3750/
> This website has information about the five senses, a glossary of senses-related words, and an activity page.

Source Notes

21 Carla McClain, "Plastic Heart from UMC Helped Build an Ironman," *Arizona Daily Star*, February 3, 2005, http://www.azstarnet.com/sn/health/59748.php (May 10, 2006).

29 Lyn Kolsteren, e-mail message to author, March 18, 2005.

31 Dale Hylton, e-mail message to author, March 29, 2005.

34 Grace Jango, telephone interview with author, March 21, 2005.

34 Dora Jango, telephone interview with author, March 22, 2005.

Photo Acknowledgments

The images in this book are used with the permission of:

© Royaly-Free/CORBIS, pp. 1 (background), 2–48 even pages (background); © Fotoware/The Image Works, pp. 4, 30 (both); © Berkeley Robotics and Human Engineering Laboratory, p. 5; © Frederick M. Brown/Getty Images, p. 6; © Reuters/CORBIS, p. 7; © MPI/Hulton Archive/Getty Images, p. 8; Courtesy Motion Control, Inc., p. 9; © Princess Margaret Rose Orthopaedic Hospital/Photo Researchers, Inc., p. 10; Courtesy of Otto Bock Health Care, p. 11 (both); © AP/Wide World Photos, p. 12 (top); © Roger Ressmeyer/CORBIS, p. 12 (bottom); © Lester Lefkowitz/CORBIS, p. 13; © Ed Kashi/CORBIS, pp. 15, 34; © Samuel Ashfield/Photo Researchers, Inc., p. 16; PhotoDisc Royalty Free by Getty Images, p. 17; Business Wire, p. 20; © Henry Leutwyler/Life Magazine/ Time & Life Pictures/Getty Images, p. 21; © Michele S. Graham/Photo Researchers, Inc., p. 22 (top); © Greer & Associates, Inc./SuperStock, p. 22 (bottom left); © SIU/Visuals Unlimited, p. 22 (bottom right); © Stephen Dunn/Getty Images, p. 23; "Pump Wear, Inc." www.pumpwearinc.com , p. 24; © Clouds Hill Imaging Ltd./ Photo Researchers, Inc., p. 27 (left); © Anatomical Travelogue/Photo Researchers, Inc., p. 27 (right); © Spike Mafford/Getty Images, p. 28 (center); © Digital Vision/Getty Images, p. 28 (bottom); © Annabella Bluesky/ Photo Researchers, Inc., p. 29; © Torsten Blackwood/AFP/Getty Images, p. 31; Courtesy of F. A. Mussa-Ivaldi, p. 36 (both); Courtesy of Duke University Photography, p. 38 (both); © 20th Century Fox/The Kobal Collection, p. 39; © James King-Holmes/Photo Researchers, Inc., p. 40 (left); © Yoshikazu Tsuno/AFP/Getty Images, p. 40 (right); © Erik Viktor/Photo Researchers, Inc., p. 41. Diagrams by Laura Westlund, pp. 18, 28, 32.

Front cover (clockwise from top): © Berkeley Robotics and Human Engineering Laboratory (Exoskeleton); Courtesy Motion Control, Inc. (Prosthetic Arm); Courtesy Starkey Laboratories; © David S. Holloway/Getty Images; © Royalty-Free/CORBIS (background). Back Cover: © Royalty-Free/CORBIS

About the Author

Judith Jango-Cohen has traveled for years as a naturalist and photographer. She was also a science teacher, so scientific topics are her favorite subjects. Among her forty-one children's books are titles that have been recommended by the National Science Teacher's Association, chosen for the Children's Literature Choice List, and named a Best Children's Book of the Year by the Children's Book Committee at Bank Street College. You can find out more about her books and school visits at www.jangocohen.com.